FISHING
FOR KIDS
A COMPLETE GUIDE

By Tony R. Smith

Welcome to the world of fishing. You are about to join the ranks of thousands of like-minded anglers – some of the best conservationists on earth. Each of them started right where you are today...as a beginner. You will learn from experience and from friends and family. You will share lifetime memories with them.

Parents realize how important time management has become. Families must plan to enjoy family activities and events. You are beginning an activity that takes practice and patience to become successful. Try to keep this in mind...fishing is a life-long sporting challenge. It is one you will be able to pass to your children and future generations. It is time well spent.

Fish is definitely good food, and time spent with family is a treasure, but time spent fishing is also healthy for you. Stress is a major factor in today's world, and stress relief can not be better defined than a day's fishing. Fishing also helps each individual develop a sense of stewardship for aquatic resources that support fish and responsibility to maintain a healthy environment.

You'll enjoy fishing. The information in this book will help you find the fishing gear you will need. Don't forget your positive attitude, friendly nature, and a good friend. You'll soon find that you are hooked on a lifetime of enjoyment.

TABLE OF CONTENTS

Welcome --- i

Table of Contents -- 1

Introduction -- 2

Safety Equipment --- 3

Basic Fishing Skills -- 4

Section 1. TACKLE --- 4

   Fishing Pole Selection --- 4

   Assembly -- 6

   Knot Tying -- 6

Section 2. CASTING PRACTICE ----------------------------------- 9

   Body Position -- 9

   Beginning Casting -- 10

   Advanced Casting -- 11

Section 3. FISHING TECHNIQUES -------------------------------- 12

   Choosing Appropriate Tackle ---------------------------------- 12

   Adjusting the Drag --- 14

   Holding the Pole -- 14

   Retrieving -- 14

   Setting the Hook -- 14

   Playing the Fish --- 15

Section 4. GOING FISHING ------------------------------------- 15

   Think Safety --- 15

   Choosing Where to Fish -- 16

   What Fish Live Here? --- 18

   Choosing Bait --- 20

Section 5. CARING FOR THE CATCH ---------------------------- 21

   Catch and Release -- 21

   Catch and Keep --- 22

   Cleaning Your Catch -- 23

   Final Touches for Fillets --------------------------------------- 29

   Caring for Cleaned Fish -- 29

Glossary --- 30

  Bonus Content--- 32

INTRODUCTION

This short course is designed to give basic fishing knowledge to those with limited fish- ing experience and to stimulate anglers to learn more. The objective is to help the new angler have safer and more enjoyable fishing trips. Once they learn the fundamentals, this guide will be a handy reference as beginning anglers move for- ward in fishing. Numbered pictures are presented with the text. A glossary of fishing terms is found on the inside back cover.

Safety Equipment

When people are learning a new activity, personal safety has to be the first consideration. Safety equipment includes:

- Personal Floatation Device (PFD) or life jackets. While PFDs must be readily available for each person on a boat, they are equally important when you are fishing from shore. PFDs are strongly recommended for all anglers when fishing near deep or swift water. If leading a group of youngsters in these conditions, they should be mandatory.
- Throwable floatation with a rope attached is recommended if several new anglers are fishing in the same area.
- Suntan lotion with a minimum SPF 15 is recommended.
- Insect repellent and medicine may be needed for stings or bites.
- Sunglasses protect the eyes from glare and from errant fish hooks.
- A hat protects the wearer from flying lures.
- Wear appropriate clothes and protective gear for anticipated weather.

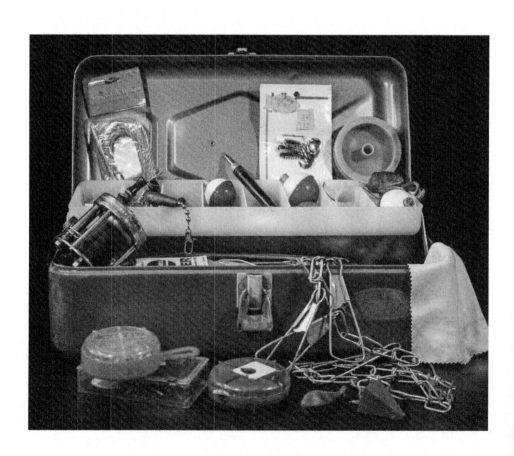

Basic Fishing Skills

Participants who use this information will be introduced to the various types of equipment, tackle, and learning experiences. After learning how to assemble the fishing equipment and stringing the line, budding anglers will experience knot tying and simple techniques used to cast. They will then learn to hook appropriate bait to catch common fish. In all cases, we hope these lessons lead to fishing adventures.

As you plan to go fishing, you need to know where to place your bait. Habitat features that typically attract fish will be described. We certainly hope you catch fish, so fish handling, cleaning and preparation of the catch will also be discussed.

Section 1. TACKLE

Fishing tackle is the connection between the angler and the fish. The fishing tackle is necessary both to get the lure or bait to the fish and to get the fish to the angler.

A. Fishing Pole Selection

Fishing poles are named for the reel (or lack of reel) that holds the fishing line. Each type of fishing reel has an appropriate fishing rod that goes with it.

1. **Pole and Line**. (*Figure 1*). The simplest gear is a pole with fishing line attached to the end. It is used with a float and hook or lure. This gear is simple yet very effective for fish in shallow water.

2. **Spincast Gear**. (*Figure 2*). Spincast gear, a simple rod with a reel, is usually the appropriate rod and reel for beginning anglers. The fishing line comes out of a hole in the reel cover. The thumb button releases the line or stops the line from going too far. Spincast gear is used to cast light to medium size lures.

3. **Spinning Gear**. (*Figure 3*). Spinning reels can cast farther than spincast gear. The fishing line on a spinning reel is exposed, and the index finger is used to release the line and to control the line. Various spinning gear is used for casting very light to heavy lures.

4. **Baitcast Gear**. (*Figure 4*). Baitcast gear has more control than spinning gear. In a casting reel, the fishing line rotates the spool as the line comes off the spool. During the cast, the thumb is used to release the line and for control. Bait casting gear is used to cast moderate to very heavy weights farther than other reels.

5. **Fly**. (*Figure 5*).A fly rod works differently than other rods. In fly fishing the lure is carried by the line instead of the lure carrying the line. The fly rod casts very light lures typically made of feathers, fur or fibers. Fly fishing is not difficult, but it normally takes training and practice to learn properly.

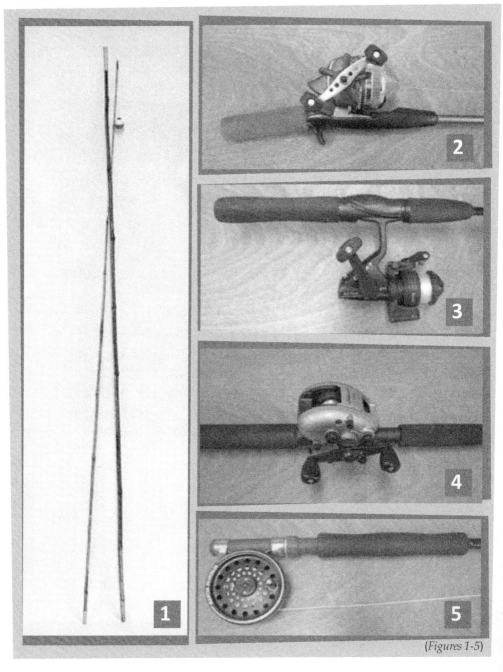

(*Figures 1-5*)

B. Assembly

When you buy a new fishing pole, it usually requires assembly.

- Remove all parts from the package.
- Put the sections of the rod together with all guides lined up in a straight line.
- Different reels attach in different ways. Loosen the attachment device and place the reel into the seat of the rod with front of the reel pointed toward the guides.
- Tighten the attachment device snugly but do not use too much pressure, as plastic parts may break or threads will strip.
- Some reels come without line. Follow package directions if line needs to be added.
- Release line from reel and thread line through all guides.
- Attach appropriate tackle for intended fishing or casting.

C. Knot Tying

Tying quality knots is the single most important skill that should be learned. A knot that connects the hook or lure to your line is the most important knot to learn. There are several that work well, such as Improved Clinch, Palomar, Uni, and Surgeon knots. This pamphlet will describe these knots with diagrams for tying them.

Other knots are used for special purposes such as connecting fishing lines together. When you buy fishing line, maintain the manufacturer's pamphlet in your tackle box. You should pick a favorite knot and master the skill of tying it.

Improved Clinch Knot

The improved clinch knot is a basic knot for beginning anglers to use with monofilament line. To tie an improved clinch knot:

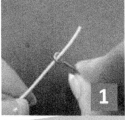

1. pass the line through the eye of the hook,

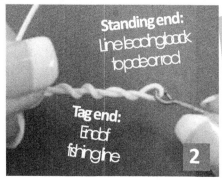

Standing end:
Line leading back to reel or rod

Tag end:
End of fishing line

2. make five turns around the standing end of the line (more for lighter line),

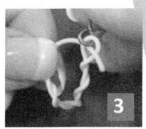

3. pass the tag end through the "tear drop" loop above eye,
4. pass the tag end through the "big loop",
5. moisten the line and slide the knot tight against the eye.

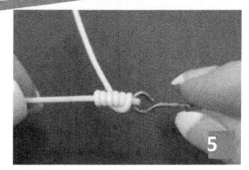

Palomar Knot

The palomar knot is also a good knot for beginning anglers, as it is strong and easy to tie. To tie a palomar knot:

1. double about 4 inches of line and pass loop through hook or lure eye, (for small openings, pass line through, then pass through in opposite direction creating the loop)
2. tie an overhand knot with loop and doubled line,
3. pass hook or lure completely through line loop, and
4. moisten line and pull knot tight against the eye.

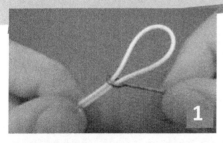

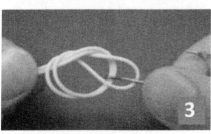

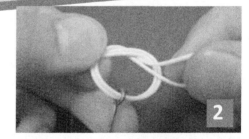

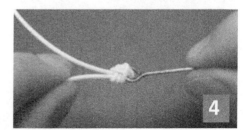

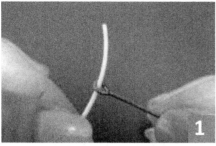

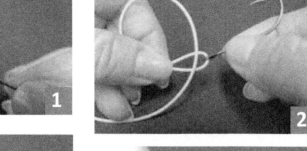

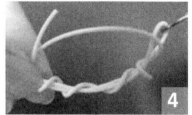

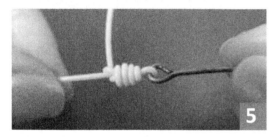

Uni-Knot

The uni knot is a third option. It is a very reliable knot for tying hooks to line or flies to leaders. To tie the uni knot:

1. pass the line through the eye of the hook,
2. pull 5-6 inches through the eye and form a loop above the standing line,
3. take the tag end around the standing line and inside the loop four to five times,
4. bring the tag end out the top of the loop,
5. pull on the standing line to tighten the knot.

Surgeon's End Loop

The surgeons end loop is used to tie a loop at the end of a fishing line. To tie a surgeons end loop:

1. double about 4 inches of line and tie an overhand knot with it,

8 -

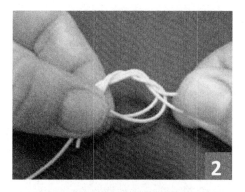

2. bring doubled end through the loop once again, and
3. hold both the standing end and tag end and pull loop to tighten knot.

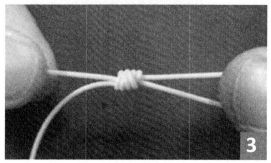

For all knots, when the knot is complete, cut the tag end cleanly about ¼ inch from the knot and discard the tag end properly.

Section 2. CASTING PRACTICE

(Group activity explained, works for individuals)

A. Body position

Before using a fishing rod, new anglers should understand body position and hand and arm action.

• Start with caster's feet and shoulders square to the target. This is accomplished by having them point the toes of both feet at the target area.

• Next, toss a tennis or ping pong ball overhand (action similar to throwing a dart) a few feet for accuracy (hit my hand). Make sure they keep their shoulders square.

This is the desired body and arm action for accurate casting. Release of the ball is at a similar position as thumb release when casting. Now transition to fishing rods, with spincast rods recommended.

B. Beginning Casting

When learning to cast a fishing pole for the first time, it is recommended to have new anglers tie on a casting plug without hooks, using newly learned knots.

- As safety is an important habit to establish, each person should check the immediate area around and above him/her to be sure each caster has plenty of space.
- Reel in line so casting plug hangs a few inches from the tip of the rod.
- Line all casters across the casting area.
- Have all anglers point the fishing rod at an object on the horizon with the hands comfortably at the waist. (Some youth may have difficulty holding the pole with one hand, so the rod may be held with one hand or two.) This is the 3 o'clock position.

- Have each caster raise the rod to 1:30 clock position (normal release point), push the push button with their thumb, and practice sliding thumb off the button (release the line). If line does not come out, pull line slightly to start. Reel the plug back to original position, a few inches from the tip. Repeat as necessary.

- When ready to cast, the casters should slowly move the rods to point them slightly behind the shoulder of the casting arm, the 11 o'clock position. Hands should be slightly above and in front of the shoulder with forearms nearly straight up and down. Hold this position momentarily to concentrate.

-10

With the thumb of the casting arm, push and hold the push button on the reel. To cast, the hand should go up slightly and forward as the caster extends the arm.

By rotating the wrist, move the rod back toward the 3 o'clock position in a quick motion, extending the arm forward.

Slide the thumb off the button at the same point as they originally released the ball (approximately 1: 30 clock position).

Stop the fishing rod with it pointed slightly above the original target.

If the lure went too high and fell short, angler released the button too soon. If the lure went too low and fell short, the button was released too late.

C. Advanced Casting

When anglers advance from spincasting to spinning or baitcast- ing, the overhead cast is the easiest cast with which to start. However, after mastering basic casting with each type of equipment, the angler needs to vary the position of the rod for different situations. Advanced casting can include a quick transition from 3 o'clock to 11 o'clock and back forward (constant motion) to add the rod's "catapult" action.

A. Choosing Appropriate Tackle

Terminal tackle is the tackle between the fish and the rod.

Hooks. Hooks keep fish attached to your line. Hooks must be kept sharp. Hooks come in many sizes and types. Ask your bait and tackle dealer what is appropriate for the species you are trying to catch and the bait you are using. The size fishing line or leader you are using should be dependent on the size hook you are using. If you get nibbles, but you are not catching them, switch to a smaller hook.

Snaps and swivels. Most hooks and lures are more effective without snaps or snap-swivels attached. Crank baits (wobbling lures) are the exception. If you are trying a variety of lures, a small but strong snap will make changing lures easier. A swivel or three-way swivel can be used to attach a dropper that keeps bait or lures off the bottom.

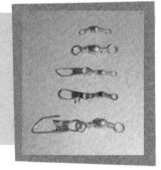

Weights or Sinkers. Only enough weight should be used to cast the bait and keep it at the desired depth. More weight will be needed in windy weather or swift water. To prevent losing a fish, weights should be attached carefully, especially when they clamp on the fishing line directly between the hook and the angler.

Floats. Floats are used to keep baits off the bottom and to assist with detecting a bite. The float should be just large enough to do the job; if the float is too large, the fish will feel it and may not become hooked.

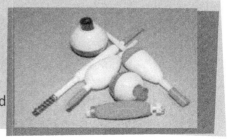

Other tackle that is helpful in fishing (*Figure 10*) includes a tackle box to hold all equipment. A sharpening stone keeps hooks and knives sharp. A lure retriever frees lures. A rag keeps your hands clean. Fingernail clippers or scissors safely cut fishing line. A pair of long nose pliers with wire cutters is useful for holding and removing fish hooks.

A fish basket keeps smaller fish alive until you finish your fishing trip. Some anglers land fish with a net after they are hooked; landing nets are more critical for large fish, fish with spines such as catfish, and fish with sharp teeth such as musky, sauger and walleye. A cooler with ice keeps your catch fresh. A thin, flexible fillet knife makes it easier to clean fish. An inch ruler measures fish to verify legal length. An angler's diary helps you become a better angler by reminding you of how fish were caught, what the weather was like, and what the fish were eating.

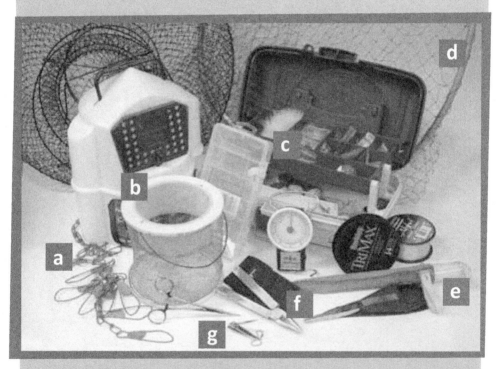

Figure 10. Tackle that is helpful to the beginning angler: (a) stringers or floating fish baskets can help keep fish fresh, (b) bait containers, (c) tackle box, (d) a landing net is useful with large fish, (e) a fillet knife is designed specifically for fish, (f) long nose pliers are a useful all-around tool, (g) finger nail clippers for clipping line

B. Adjusting the Drag

See the reel diagram for your reel to find the drag adjustment. There are two ways to adjust the drag. One is to tighten the drag (toward the + sign) until the line can be pulled directly from the reel with some resistance. (If a friend is helping, have him/her pull line from the pole, while you hold the pole as if fighting a fish). The other way is to use a weight that is equal to 1/3 the tensile strength of your line. Attach the weight to the line as if fishing and adjust the drag until the weight can just be lifted from the floor with the pole.

balance point (fulcrum)
Figure 11

C. Holding the Pole

Every pole has a balance point (fulcrum) with the reel and lure attached (*Figure 11*). If the angler holds the pole at this point, leverage to fight the fish is greater than when the pole is held behind this point. This also allows the angler to place the end of the pole (butt end) against the belt to fight larger fish.

D. Retrieving

This is the act of bringing a bait or lure back to the angler (*Figure 12*). After casting, live and prepared bait are often left in one spot until retrieved. Some baits and most artificial lures are most effectively presented while retrieving. The retrieve can be slow or fast; it can be steady or erratic.

Figure 12

E. Setting the Hook

Once the fish bites the lure, the hook must be pulled into the fish to hold the fish. If using barbed hooks, pull hard enough to pull the barb into the jaw. Then the fish can be brought to the angler (*Figure 13*). When the fish bites, the fishing rod should be quickly pulled up to set the hook into the fish. The force needed to set the hook depends on the rod, line, species of fish, and the lure or bait used. For example, a crappie caught on a light line and minnows will need only a gentle lifting of the rod to set the hook. A bass angler, fishing with heavier line and the hook buried in a plastic worm, will need a vigorous rod sweep to force the hook through the worm and into the bony mouth of a bass.

Figure 13

F. Playing the Fish

After setting the hook, the line should be kept tight so the fish will not shake the hook loose. The fishing rod should be held between a 10 o'clock and a 12 o'clock position. Allow the rod to fight the fish. Properly adjusted drag will allow the line to release prior to breaking. Large fish must be moved by a pumping action; a large fish is repeatedly pulled toward the angler with the rod. After pulling the rod to the 12 o'clock position to move the fish, reel in the fishing line to maintain a tight line as the rod is lowered back to the 10 o'clock position.

Section 4. GOING FISHING

A. Think Safety

When taking a new person fishing, it is important they have an enjoyable experience. Therefore, find a pond, lake or stream that is safe and easily fished. As they learn and advance their skills, new challenges can be introduced; however, always include the safety equipment required for the new situation.

B. Choosing Where to Fish

Some fishing areas are better than others. The quality of fish- ing depends upon the water's productivity, the fish species present, and the size of the fish present. Productive water has more fish than unproductive water; up to a point, the greener the water is, the more productive the water. In some waters, undesirable fish compete with desirable fish. Fishing is better in a lake with a high proportion of the right size fish. Check the fishing forecast for predicted "hot spots."

Habitat is the key to fish survival, and fishing near habitat will result in more bites. Stumps, weed beds, and man-made fish attrac- tors are all good examples of fish habitat. During summer, fish can be found near fishing or boating docks, as they prefer shaded areas.

farm ponds

In streams and rivers, anglers focus on riffles, the swift areas that bring food into the deep, slower portions. Fish congregate in this area and feed more actively as water begins to rise and carry more food. Also you should try areas that fish use for resting. Fish rest in areas where the current is slowed by rocks, trees or in eddies near the swift water.

Current attracts fish in reservoirs as well as in streams. Current flow rates are higher under bridges; therefore, bank fishing from highway bridge approaches or near bridges from a boat can be good. Safety should be a top priority in these bank areas, including the use of life jackets.

The areas below dams are called tailwaters. As fish migrate up river to spawn, they sometimes encounter a dam. Since many fish are migrating together, fish are concentrated. Fishing can be very good

city lakes

at specific times of the year. Caution should be used in these areas, including the use of life jackets. If fishing these areas from a boat, maintain appropriate distance from the discharge areas for safety and as required by law.

    1. Private Waters. Private ponds, streams and rivers are often excellent places to fish. The permission of the owner is required to fish water when you are walking on private property. A few simple courte-

streams

tailwaters

sies will help you get invited back.
- If you desire to keep any fish from a stocked pond, ask how many, what species, and what size fish you may keep.
- Ask the owner if they would like any of your catch.
- Ask before you bring anyone with you.
- Do not litter.
- Close all gates behind you.
- Report any problems immediately to the owner.

    2. Public Waters. Larger lakes are normally managed by public entities such as the Army Corps of Engineers, Tennessee Valley Authority, state wildlife agency or perhaps a power company. Public access points allow anglers boating and fishing access. For more information contact the information division of your state fish and wildlife agency.

C. What Fish Live Here?

    Most ponds have a combination of large-mouth bass, bluegill, redear sunfish, and channel catfish. Larger lakes will have more variety. Streams and rivers will have many of the native fishes, plus a few introduced species.

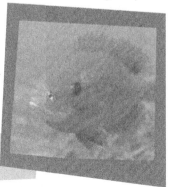

Bluegill

Smallmouth Bass

Pumpkinseed

Largemouth Bass

Rock Bass

Check the fish identification booklet from your state fish and wildlife agency to find the proper habitat to fish for a given species.

D. Choosing Bait

Every angler has a favorite bait or lure to catch fish. It works because that lure is on the line most often. By sharing information with new anglers, we help them be successful while learning the variety of fishing techniques.

Live bait simulates food items that fish normally eat. Bait that is alive and moving after you hook it will catch more fish. Some bait is available year-round and some is seasonal. See your state's fish ID book for ideas on what baits work for which fish.

Meal worm - Insert a size 6 - 8 hook into the underside of the meal worm (note tiny legs) near one end. Run the hook inside and bring the point of the hook out near the opposite end.

Red worm - Run the hook, usually a size 6 - 8, through the worm about ½ inch from one end. Go through the worm about every inch leaving ½ inch wriggling at the other end.

Night crawler - Use larger hooks, such as size 2. Can either be hooked like a red worm or in one spot only. To give the worm a natural look, run the hook inside the worm to hide the shank and barely bring the point of the hook through the skin of the worm.

Minnow - Size of hook varies depending on size of minnow and target fish. Two methods: 1. Run hook through both lips of the minnow. 2. Run hook through the back behind the dorsal (top) fin (be careful not to pierce the spine).

Cricket - Use a size 8, long shank hook. Looking at the back of the cricket, run the point of the hook under the sheath behind the head. Bring the point of the hook out behind the sheath.

Artificial lures - If you do not want to use live bait, you can select from a variety of artificial lures.

Section 5. CARING FOR THE CATCH

Before your fishing trip begins, you should plan how you will care for your catch. The decision to catch and release or keep should be made before you catch your first fish.

A. Catch and Release

If the decision is to release fish, all fish should be handled as little as possible and fish should be returned to the water as quickly as possible. The best method is to hold the fish in the water, reach to the fish and remove the hook with needle nose pliers (*Figure 14*). If you need to remove the fish from the water, return it as quickly as possible. In warmer water, moving the fish back and forth with water entering the mouth will help the fish recover more quickly. However, in some cases, fish caught from deep in a lake (cool water) can not swim back down to the cool water due to air bladder expansion. They may not survive if released in warm surface water, and anglers should consider keeping legal fish rather than releasing them.

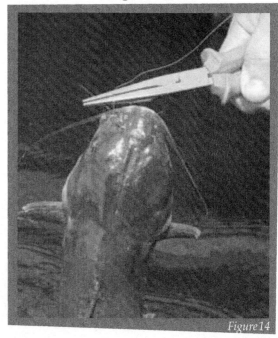

Figure 14

B. Catch and Keep.

Anglers who choose to keep and eat the fish they catch should refer to their state's annual fishing guide for the latest updates on creel and size limits plus fish comsumption advisories. By knowing how many fish you intend to keep and what size (selective release), you can plan for other equipment. Many fish are kept in floating fish baskets or on stringers; however these work best in cooler weather. In warmer water, fish tend to die quickly due to stress from heat and from being caught. All fish are best when they are kept fresh on ice. To keep your cooler clean and to keep fish out of the water, use a plastic bag to isolate your catch.

C. Cleaning Your Catch.

After you leave the water with your catch, you want to properly prepare it for eating. There are two different ways to clean your catch: filleting and dressing.

1.Filleting (*Figures 15-19*) involves cutting the edible part of the fish away from the inedible part; no bones are left in the edible portion.

2.Dressing (*Figures 20-22*) implies taking off parts that cannot be eaten, and most bones are left with the edible portion. Some fish, like catfish, have a skin that must be removed (*Figures 23* and *24*). Other fish have to be scaled with a knife or a spoon (*Figure 20*).

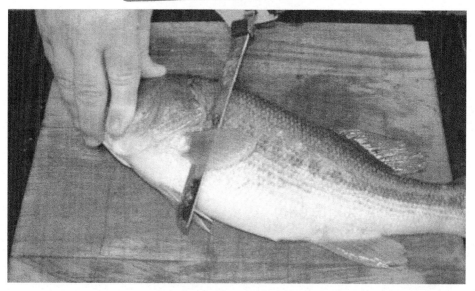

Figure 15. Filleting fish, such as bass, removes all bones from the meat. To fillet a bass, place the fish on its side on a firm, flat surface. Make a cut behind the gill plate from the top of the fish to the belly and into the flesh to the backbone. Do not cut through the backbone.

Figure 16. Without removing the knife turn the blade toward the tail, cut through the ribs, and continue on the tail, closely following the backbone as a guide. Do not cut through the skin completely at the tail, but leave a half to one inch intact.

Figure 17. Flip the fillet over, skin side down, and insert the blade between the skin and the meat.

24 -

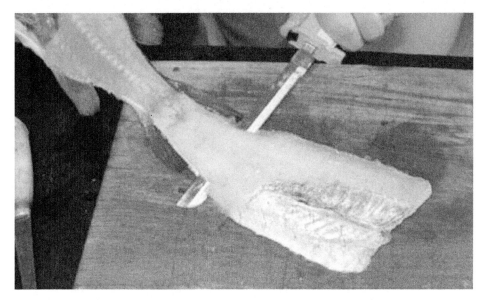

Figure 18. With a sawing motion, follow the inside of the skin closely with the blade and cut the meat away from the skin.

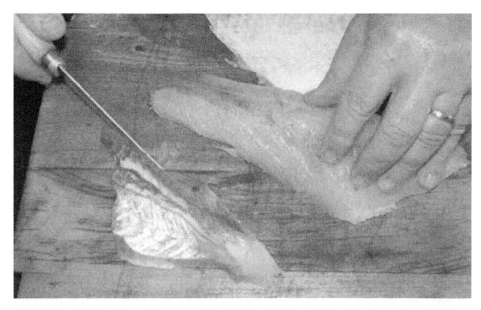

Figure 19. Cut the ribs away from the skinless fillet. Repeat the steps for the other side of the fish.

DRESSING

Figure 20. Small fish, such as bream (sunfish), are usually dressed. Dressing a fish leaves some of the bones in the meat, but less meat is lost during the cleaning process.

Figure 21. To dress a small fish, place the fish on its side on a firm, flat surface. Use one hand to hold it in place by the head. Scrape the scales from the tail toward the head by using a fish scaler, spoon, or dull knife. Remove the scales on both sides of the body.

Figure 22. Use a fillet knife to cut along both sides of the dorsal fin. Grasp the dorsal fin and pull forward to remove. Spines should pull out with fin. Repeat process to remove the anal fin and spines.

Figure 23. Cut off the head immediately behind the gills and remove the organs. Wash in cold, clean water. The fish is now ready to freeze or cook.

Figure 24. Some fish, such as catfish, are usually skinned. To skin a catfish, first remove the spines to prevent puncture of a hand or finger. Cut through the skin around the head and pectoral fins. Do not penetrate the body cavity.

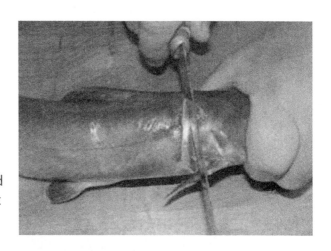

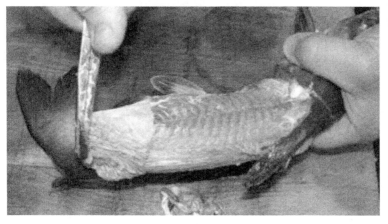

Figure 25. Using a pair of pliers, pull the skin away from the meat, working from the head toward the tail. Break or cut the head away from the backbone and remove the internal organs.

Figure 26. The finished product, ready for the skillet.

D. Final Touches for Fillets

Many fish have a dark strip on the "skin side" of the fillet. This is what is left of a blood vessel that took blood to the tail. It is also a place where fat has been stored, and fat is associated with some of the pollut- ants that accumulate in fish flesh.

Using a fillet knife, lift that fat and dark area out.

(1) Make a "v-cut" the full length of the fillet from both sides of the dark area.
(2) Now lift out the dark meat out, gently cutting underneath it, and discard that portion.

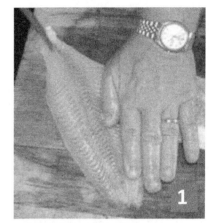

Next look on both edges of the fil- let for white or yellow fat. Trim that fat and your fillet is ready for your fish fry!

Eating fish, even fish from an area listed in fish advisories, is a choice you make as an angler. By limiting your consumption rate, selecting smaller fish to eat (less time to accu- mulate pollutants), removing as much of the potentially polluted flesh (fat) as possible, and cooking it properly, you lower your risk dramatically. For more information on fish advisories, see your state's fishing guide.

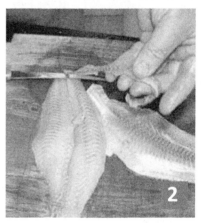

E. Caring for Cleaned Fish

Once fish are cleaned, they should be washed thoroughly, then frozen immediately or refrigerated and cooked within three days. Frozen fish may develop freezer burn unless they are tightly wrapped or frozen in water. When freezing fish in water, you should use just enough water to cover them. Plastic freezer bags work well for fillets, if they can be sealed without leaking.

There are numerous cookbooks that have a variety of recipes and methods for cooking fish for the table. By trying many different ways of fixing fish, the angler finds those dishes that best suit individual tastes.

GLOSSARY

bait - usually refers to something natural or live that is used to attract fish to bite. The terms bait and lure may be used interchangeably.

bite - when a fish tries to take a bait (or lure). Also called a strike.

casting - the skill of propelling a bait or lure into the water.

cleaning - preparing your catch for eating.

conservation - the wise use of natural resources.

creel limit - the number of fish an angler can keep in a day.

dressed - fish prepared for eating complete with bones.

dropper - a separate line tied onto the main line near the hook. It is used to attach a weight to a separate line or to fish two hooks.

fillet - cleaning a fish by cutting the edible portion from the bones.

fishing line - special flexible fiber; connects fishing reel to the hook.

float, bobber or cork - maintains bait at given depth, indicates bites.

habitat - combination of food, water, shelter and space that attracts given animal.

land - bringing the fish to the land or to a net for capture.

leader - the piece of line attached to the hook.

lunker - a large specimen of a species of fish.

lure - usually refers to man-made bait used to entice fish to bite.

monofilament - fishing line with a single strand of material.

multifilament - fishing line that is several strands woven together.

playing - process of bringing a fish to the angler so it can be landed.

reel - a device that holds and retrieves fishing line.

rod - a pole with guides that is used to cast a lure or bait.

selective harvest - personal ethics that includes reduced harvest within established legal size and creel limits.

setting the hook - pulling the rod up sharply when a fish bites.

sinker - used to help cast or help sink the bait or lure; a weight.

slot limit - a limit to protect fish between specified sizes. Usually extends life of predators or reduces number of small fish.

snap, swivel or snap-swivel - a small metal device tied onto fishing line; used to quickly attach lures to the line. Keeps line from twisting.

strike - when a fish takes or tries to take a lure (or bait).

structure - any area that causes fish to be concentrated.

tailwater - area below a reservoir.

terminal tackle - placement of tackle at the end of the line.

LARGEMOUTH BASS

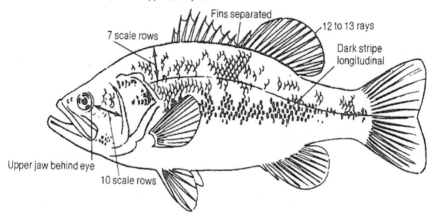

Good bait: Minnows, Grasshoppers, Crayfish

Fins separated

12 to 13 rays

Dark stripe longitudinal

7 scale rows

Upper jaw behind eye

10 scale rows

SMALLMOUTH BASS

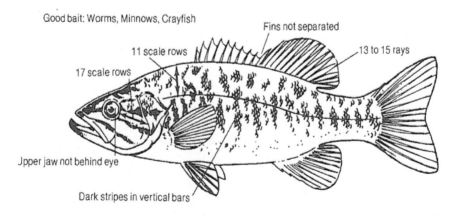

Good bait: Worms, Minnows, Crayfish

Fins not separated

13 to 15 rays

11 scale rows

17 scale rows

Jpper jaw not behind eye

Dark stripes in vertical bars

SUNFISH

Most sunfish do not grow much larger than 10 inches long, but they fight hard and are fun to catch. There are several types of sunfish, each with slightly different body characteristics (see below). Sunfish are the most common fish caught and are the easiest to catch. Typical baits used are worms, crickets, grasshoppers and artificial flies. Very small hooks with live bait and bobbers are normally used by fishermen to catch sunfish. Sunfish are usually caught in and around brush or trees in the water and weed beds close to shore. Best times of the year to catch sunfish are the spring or fall, but sunfish are usually "biting" most of the year.

Bluegill

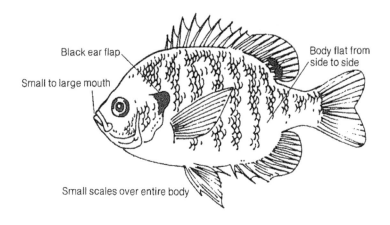

Black ear flap

Small to large mouth

Body flat from side to side

Small scales over entire body

Good bait: Worms, Grasshoppers, Crickets

Greensunfish

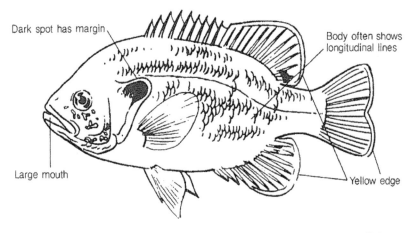

Dark spot has margin

Body often shows longitudinal lines

Large mouth

Yellow edge

White Crappie

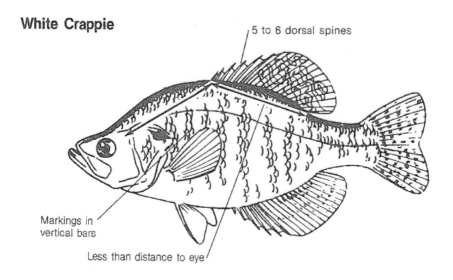

5 to 6 dorsal spines

Markings in
vertical bars

Less than distance to eye

Black Crappie

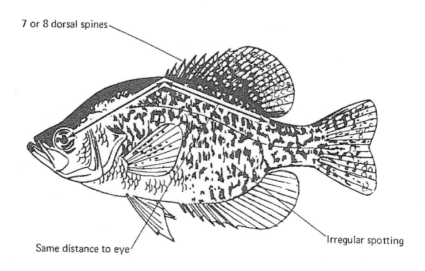

7 or 8 dorsal spines

Same distance to eye

Irregular spotting

Two species of crappie (black and white) occur in most large lakes, river lakes and many inland lakes within Illinois. Color patterns vary from dark splotches arranged in vertical bands on the white crappie to irregular dark splotches on the black crappie. Still fishing is the most common method used to fish for crappie. A small hook and lively minnow with a bobber and split shot weight or a feathered jig moved up and down are good ways to catch crappie.

White Bass

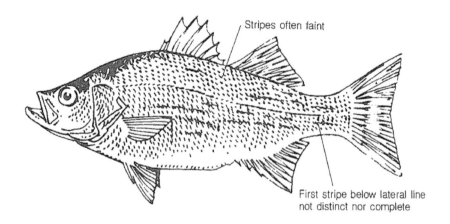

Stripes often faint

First stripe below lateral line not distinct nor complete

Yellow Bass

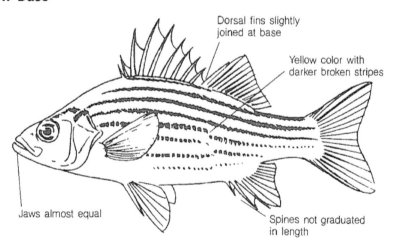

Dorsal fins slightly joined at base

Yellow color with darker broken stripes

Jaws almost equal

Spines not graduated in length

Both white and yellow bass are true freshwater bass. Yellow Bass, which do not attain the size of White Bass, are more abundant. Fishermen will often group these two species together and commonly refer to them as "stripers." However, the true Striped Bass is their larger ocean-going cousin which has adapted very well to inland freshwater lakes and rivers, and has been stocked in some of Illinois' larger reservoirs and power plant cooling lakes. As with Walleye, White and Yellow Bass fishing begins with their spawning run. There is no apparent difference in the types of bait used, as a small minnow or jig cast into the current below rock or wood debris is effective for both species. After spawning the fish will remain schooled-up and return to the lakes at which time a small spinning lure or metallic colored spoon brings good results.

BULLHEAD CATFISH

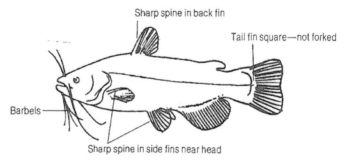

Sharp spine in back fin

Tail fin square—not forked

Barbels

Sharp spine in side fins near head

CHANNEL CATFISH

Good bait: Worms, Minnows, Liver, Prepared catfish baits

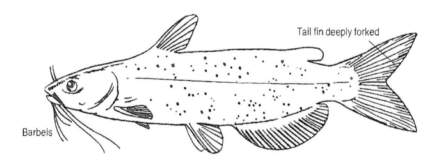

Tail fin deeply forked

Barbels

Catfish have "whiskers," or barbels. They use these and their good sense of smell to find food. They do not have scales. You must handle catfish very carefully because of the sharp spines in their fins. You can catch them close to shore. Keep your bait close to the bottom where catfish usually feed.

CARP

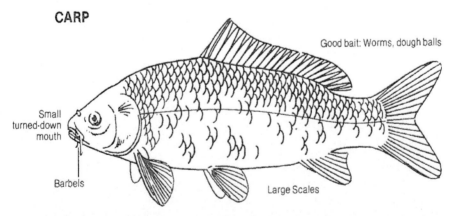

Good bait: Worms, dough balls

Small turned-down mouth

Barbels

Large Scales

Carp grow to a large size and are strong fighters to catch. They usually feed on the bottom of rivers and lakes. Their small mouths require a small hook for your bait. They like to sniff the bait and sample it before they suck it into their mouths.

-37

Muskellunge

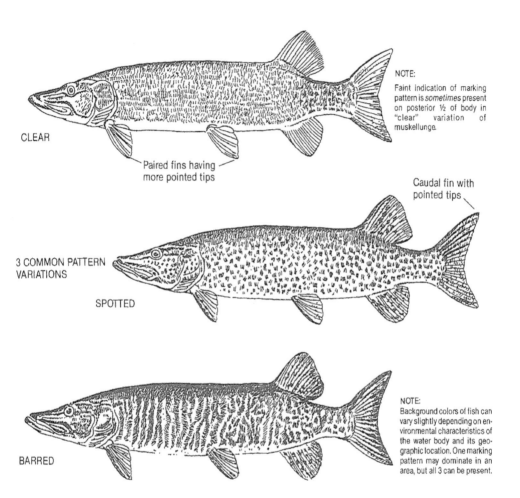

CLEAR

NOTE:
Faint indication of marking pattern is *sometimes* present on posterior ½ of body in "clear" variation of muskellunge.

Paired fins having more pointed tips

Caudal fin with pointed tips

3 COMMON PATTERN VARIATIONS

SPOTTED

BARRED

NOTE:
Background colors of fish can vary slightly depending on environmental characteristics of the water body and its geographic location. One marking pattern may dominate in an area, but all 3 can be present.

The muskellunge has forty or more common names. Among these are: Great Lakes muskellunge, muskie (musky), lunge, maskinonge, muskellunge, leopard muskellunge and tiger muskellunge. In the Cree Indian language, "mashk" means deformed and "kinonge" means pike therefore; deformed pike. The body of the muskie is long and narrow with a large head with duckbill jaws supporting large canine teeth. There are three widely accepted color patterns of pure muskellunge: clear, spotted and barred. Natural populations of muskie probably disappeared from Illinois many years ago. Today however, the muskellunge has been stocked into many lakes within Illinois. Muskies will stay in one spot unless driven out by a larger fish or caught. Large surface plugs or spoons and spinner bucktails are good artificial lures. The most commonly used live bait is a large sucker.

Northern Pike

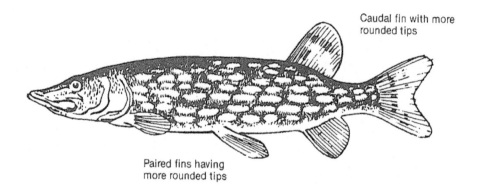

Caudal fin with more rounded tips

Paired fins having more rounded tips

The northern pike has many common names including: common pike, pickerel, great northern pike, northern, jack fish, pike, snake, snake pickerel and jack. The northern pike is very similar to the muskellunge in that it has a long and narrow body with a large head with duckbill jaws. The northern pike however; has rows of light colored, round or oval spots on its side. The northern pike occurs naturally in the northern third of Illinois and rather generally throughout the northern half of Illinois via hatchery stockings. The northern pike also occurs naturally in the Mississippi River. Large spoons and plugs are suitable artificial lures when casting or trolling. A large, lively sucker is probably the best bait when still fishing.

Location of submanibular pore on under side of lower jaw...

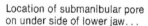

NORTHERN PIKE
5 or fewer pores

MUSKELLUNGE
6 to 9 pores

NOTE: Hybrids have 5 to 8 pores on each side of lower jaw.

Upper half of cheek and operculum with scales

MUSKELLUNGE

Entire cheek and upper half of operculum with scales

NORTHERN PIKE

NOTE: Hybrids have ⅔ or more of cheek and upper half of operculum with scales.

Tiger (Hybrid) Muskie

Caudal fin with
rounded tips

Paired fins having
rounded tips

NOTE:
Sides sometimes exhibit an
alternating pattern of stripes
and spots, or narrow paired-
bars on a light background.
Pattern *never* resembles that
of northern pike.

The tiger muskie is a hybrid due to the crossbreeding of the male of
one species and the female of another species therefore; the
northern pike and the muskellunge. The tiger muskie has a long and
narrow body with a large head with duckbill jaws supporting large
canine teeth. Coloration on the sides is usually narrow, paired-bars
on a light background. The color pattern never resembles that of a
northern pike. The tiger muskie occurs throughout Illinois as a result
of hatchery stockings. Large surface plugs, spoons and bucktails are
good artificial lures. A large, lively sucker is excellent natural bait.

YELLOW PERCH

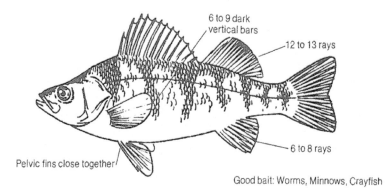

6 to 9 dark
vertical bars

12 to 13 rays

6 to 8 rays

Pelvic fins close together

Good bait: Worms, Minnows, Crayfish

The yellow perch has numerous dark vertical bars on each side of the body. The lower fins are deep yellow or orange in color, and it has small teeth on its jaws. The yellow perch usually runs in schools in both deep and shallow waters. When an experienced fisherman catches one, he tries the same spot again for others. A majority of yellow perch are caught by fishermen using live bait, either worms or minnows, still fishing with bobbers. The body of the yellow perch feels much like sandpaper due to its scales which have tiny teeth on their surface.

Walleye

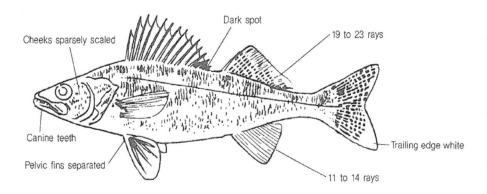

Cheeks sparsely scaled

Dark spot

19 to 23 rays

Canine teeth

Pelvic fins separated

Trailing edge white

11 to 14 rays

The separate top fins, streamline shape and large milky eye set the walleye apart from all other Illinois fish. Walleye may be found in large river systems as well as in most large Illinois lakes. Walleye are most often found in deep water, but may be caught in the spring, as they move to shallow areas to spawn. Walleye may be caught with minnows and leeches, as well as various artificial spinning and crank baits. Walleye may be the finest eating of all Illinois' fishes.

Skinning Bullhead Catfish

1 A freshly caught fish will skin easier. Cut across top of back to backbone between head and dorsal fin. A short cut toward the top fin helps tear skin.

3 Push head downward, breaking backbone where the knife made a cut across back, removing the entrails, belly flesh, and front fins along with head in one motion.

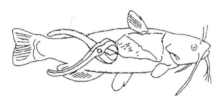

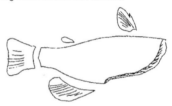

2 Pull skin toward the tail with pliers; one pull on each half should tear off skin. Second side will pick up what skin is missed on tearing off the first side.

4 If desired, the remaining fins and tail may be removed before cooking. Large catfish need more slitting of skin around head, along back, and belly before skinning.

Cleaning Trout and Salmon

1 Clean trout as soon as you can after catching it. Insert a knife at the vent and slit the belly forward to the gills.

3 Place one finger in the belly slit and gill opening and separate the side of the body from the gills and gill rakers. Insert the knife and cut the flesh loose at bottom on both sides.

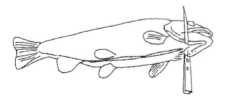

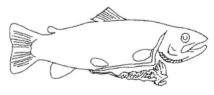

2 Insert the knife and cut at the point where the gill is attached under the throat at the V joining the lower belly to the head.

4 Stick a finger in the gill throat and tear out gills and gill rakers. Entrails will pull out with gills or remove them by hand. Remove the blood streak along spine. Remove all excess fat, especially the belly and dorsal flaps. Remove the skin on large fish. Cook so any remaining fat will be reduced.

-42

Filleting Perch and Bass

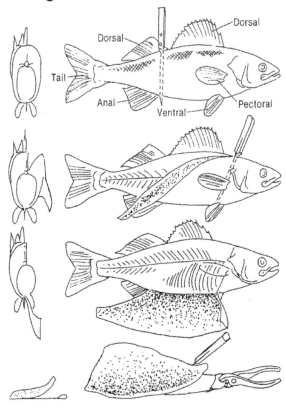

1 To save the most meat and fewest bones try this method: Cut along back on one side of dorsal fin. Insert blade all the day through body and out belly just behind vent. Slice along edge of anal fin, with blade sliding along backbone until reaching tail. Cut fillet loose and repeat on other side.

2 Slice on an angle from the top of back to belly just behind head, pectoral fin, and pelvic fin. Repeat slice on other side of body, or finish one side at a time.

3 Insert knife blade in original cut (Step 1) and slice downward freeing meat from rib cage. After working down over main part of ribs, keep cutting as close against lower ribs as possible until reaching belly. Cut through the belly, separating fillet from body.

4 Lay fillet skin flat on table. With a heavy, flat knife cut down into fillet leaving tab for holding skin. Pull on skin and use knife in a see-saw motion. Don't slice the meat off, but scrape it off with the blade and by pulling the skin.

Dressing Sunfish
(use this method for smaller fish.)

1 Using a knife or scraper, scrape off scales toward the head.

4 Continue cutting to pectoral fin. Lay fish flat and make deep cut on both sides of body behind pectoral fin.

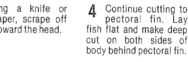

2 Hold knife parallel to fins; cut along each side of dorsal and anal fins ¼ to ½ inch deep for later removal.

5 Pull head upward to break the backbone. Head will tear loose; entrails, pectoral, and pelvic fins will be removed.

3 Hold fish upside-down with its back resting on table and cut immediately behind vent. Slip knife forward under skin.

6 Remove dorsal and anal fins, loosened in Step 2, by pulling away and forward from the body. Cut off the tail.

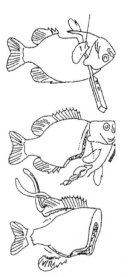

Cooking Your Catch

The basic fish cooking rules are easy to follow, even though each type of fish has individual flavor, texture, and appearance.

If you make allowances for the fat content of fish, you can successfully use any of the cooking methods for almost all species. In other words, *lean* fish (bass, sunfish) may be cooked by dry heat methods such as baking or broiling, if you baste frequently with melted butter or shortening to prevent drying. (Try combining lemon or garlic with the basting fat, or using a basting sauce.) Fish with high fat content (trout, salmon) don't have to be basted.

Avoid overcooking. The fish should be moist and tender with a delicate flavor. Overcooking causes the flesh to become increasingly dry and chewy. Fish is done when the flesh is translucent and can be easily flaked with a fork.

Don't overhandle the fish during cooking and serving. Cooked fish is delicate and will flake apart easily. Turn only once during cooking and transfer carefully to a warm platter to serve.

Never soak fresh fish in water. This causes loss of flavor and makes the flesh flabby. Wash fish quickly, drain, and dry carefully on paper towel.

Broiling

Sprinkle serving-sized portions of fish with salt and pepper. Place on preheated greased broiler pan, skin side up if skin has not been removed from fillets. Brush with melted butter. Broil about 2 inches from heat 5 to 8 minutes, or till fish flakes easily with a fork.

Baking

Rub salt on the inside and outside of the cleaned fish; place fish in a greased baking pan. Brush with melted fat (lay slices of bacon over top if desired). Bake in a moderate oven till fish flakes easily with a fork. If fish seems dry while baking, baste with drippings.

Steaming

Salt both sides of the cleaned fish. Place fish in a well-greased steamer pan and cook over boiling water till fish flakes easily with a fork. Serve at once with lemon or a sauce.

Deep fat frying

Sprinkle serving-sized portions of fish with salt and pepper. Dip fish in mixture of 1 tablespoon milk to 1 egg. Roll in bread or cracker crumbs, cornmeal, or flour. Cook fish in deep fat (375°) till golden brown. Drain on absorbent paper. Serve with lemon or sauce.

Three basic cuts of fish

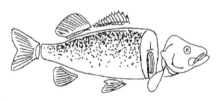

Dressed, or pan-dressed
Scaled, drawn with head, tail, and fins removed.

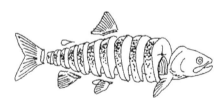

Steaked
Cross-sectional slices are cut from larger fish.

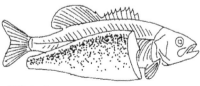

Filleted

-44

Fishing for Facts!

Fish are important to us. They provide food for millions of people and fishermen enjoy catching them for sport.

Fish are also important in the balance of nature. They eat plants and animals and, in turn, become food for plants and animals. This is called a **food chain.**

The balance of plants and animals in a lake may be upset by people catching too many fish of one kind. This is why the Illinois Department of Natural Resources sets limits on the fish you may keep. Remember, it is necessary for you to learn the fishing rules for your lake. You must take only the legal size and number of fish in order to help keep your lake healthy.

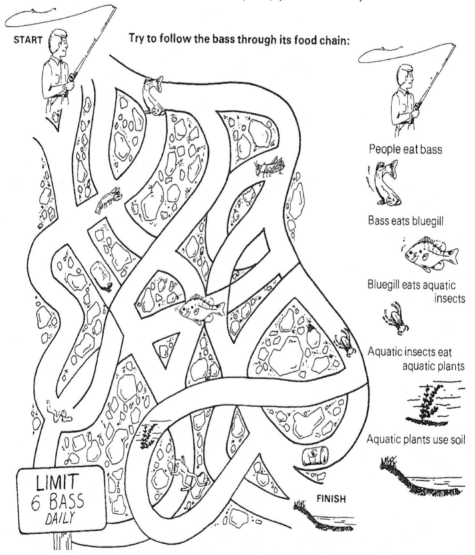

Try to follow the bass through its food chain:

START

People eat bass

Bass eats bluegill

Bluegill eats aquatic insects

Aquatic insects eat aquatic plants

Aquatic plants use soil

LIMIT
6 BASS
DAILY

FINISH

Your Friend

SPORT FISHING

Across

1. Early morning is a good _____ to fish for bass.
4. The Illinois Department of Natural Resources _____ has a bird and a tree on it.
10. A catfish with a square _____ is a bullhead.
11. Hook a grass _____ through the shoulder and into the head.
12. Attach the float to the line by pushing down _____ the button.
13. A fish fillet should not have a _____ in it.
15. A clinch knot is used to _____ a hook to the line.
17. A fishing _____ is always fun.
18. A largemouth _____ is easily recognized by its large mouth and dark blotches down its side.
19. Put worn out fishing line in the trash _____ .
20. There must be _____ water for fish to live.
21. The float may go under the _____ when a fish is biting.
26. Our clean air and water have been changed by _____ .
27. Good sportsmen throw their _____ in a can.
28. When someone catches a large fish, people say, "_____ ."
29. Carp are delicious to _____ .

Down

1. Pop-top rings and old paper cups are _____ .
2. A catfish has sharp spines in its back _____ .
3. There must be _____ water for people to live.
5. A _____ is used by a fish to take oxygen from the water.
6. All women, men and children who enjoy fishing are _____ .
7. Good sportsmen _____ our resources.
8. Conservation is _____ job.
9. Fish, forests and wild animals are natural _____ .
10. We should all work _____ to protect our natural resources.
14. A _____ is a 1- to 3-inch fish that can be used for bait.
16. One _____ of a stringer should be tied tightly to the bank.
22. Fishermen like to be fishing by 7:00 ___.___.
23. Turn the reel crank to _____ up line.
24. I'm glad I _____ my crunchy good fish.
25. A bass may _____ away if it sees you move.

(Answers on page 32.)

GOOD FISHERMEN:

1. Good fishermen **help** protect the outdoors. They don't litter – that includes not throwing away gum wrappers or orange peels and picking up all leftover bait, fish remains and other trash.

2. Good fishermen **respect** other people's privacy and territory. They fish quietly so they don't frighten fish or disturb people. And they don't crowd someone out of a fishing spot.

3. Good fishermen always **practice** safe fishing. They are careful when casting and pick up all fish hooks. If they get a fish hook caught in their skin, they get help taking it out.

4. Good fishermen **buy** and **carry** a fishing license if they are 16 years old or older.

5. Good fishermen **know** the size and number of fish it's legal to keep. Limits provide more chances for more people to catch fish.

6. Good fishermen **release** fish right away if they don't plan to eat them.

Word Lake Puzzle Answers
(from page 9)

Crossword Puzzle Answers
(from page 28)

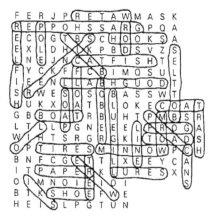

Could This Happen?

When this land was new
We thrived in great rivers,
In quiet lakes,
In rushing streams of deep woods,
In small ponds of fields and farms.

There we hatched and fed and grew
And swam in the clear, clean water.

Then people came
And came and changed the land.
People came and paved and dumped
And littered and spilled
And changed the world.

We gasped for air.
We swam to deep pools
And found them trashed and spoiled.
We looked for a place to hide and rest—
A place to breed and raise our young—
But there was none.

I swim alone!

1. What is the animal in the poem? _____
2. Were people's actions helpful to it? _____
3. Describe some things that could happen if all the water in the world suddenly became polluted.
   _____
   _____

4. How many examples of polluted water have you seen today? _____

AGE of FISH

Outer Edge
2nd Annulus
or Year Mark
1st Annulus
Focus or Center

This scale was taken from a bass in its third year. The fish was 12 inches long and grew about 6 inches its first year and 4 inches during the second year.

The year marks or annuli are formed during the winter months when the fish is growing very slowly.

Growth rates of fish vary — the better the food supply and the longer the growing season, the

-49

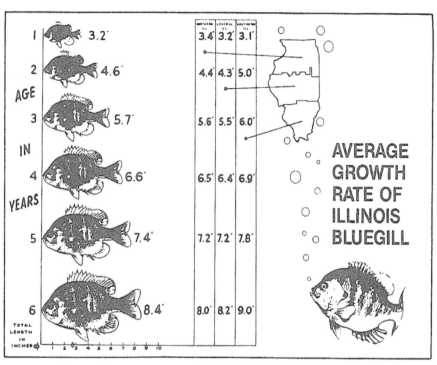

AVERAGE GROWTH RATE OF ILLINOIS BLUEGILL

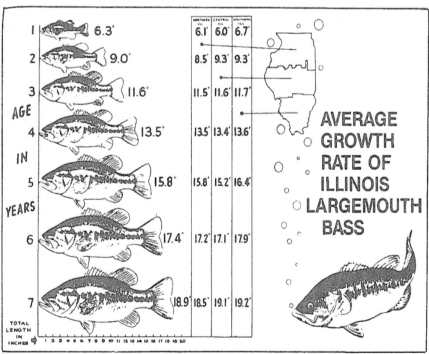

AVERAGE GROWTH RATE OF ILLINOIS LARGEMOUTH BASS

BAIT HOOK SIZES

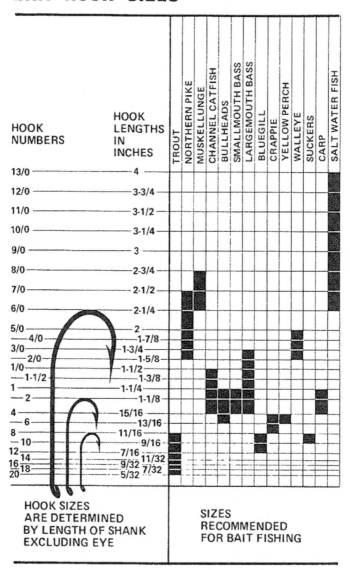

HOOK NUMBERS	HOOK LENGTHS IN INCHES	TROUT	NORTHERN PIKE	MUSKELLUNGE	CHANNEL CATFISH	BULLHEADS	SMALLMOUTH BASS	LARGEMOUTH BASS	BLUEGILL	CRAPPIE	YELLOW PERCH	WALLEYE	SUCKERS	CARP	SALT WATER FISH
13/0	4														
12/0	3-3/4														■
11/0	3-1/2														
10/0	3-1/4														■
9/0	3														
8/0	2-3/4			■											
7/0	2-1/2		■												■
6/0	2-1/4		■												
5/0	2														
4/0	1-7/8		■									■			
3/0	1-3/4														
2/0	1-5/8		■									■			
1/0	1-1/2														
1-1/2	1-3/8				■										
1	1-1/4				■	■	■								
2	1-1/8				■	■	■							■	
4	15/16					■		■							
6	13/16									■	■				
8	11/16														
10	9/16									■			■		
12	7/16	■													
14	11/32														
16	9/32	■													
18	7/32	■													
20	5/32														

HOOK SIZES
ARE DETERMINED
BY LENGTH OF SHANK
EXCLUDING EYE

SIZES
RECOMMENDED
FOR BAIT FISHING

-51

Notes

Notes

Notes

Notes

Notes

Notes

Notes

Notes

Notes

Notes

Fish Recipes

SALMON

Salmon is a superfood boasting loads of protein and healthy fats. Another bonus: Just a mere 4-oz. serving of wild salmon serves up **a full day's requirement of vitamin D**. And that same piece of fish contains over 50 percent of vital nutrients like **B12**, **niacin**, and **selenium**. Salmon also proves an impressive source of **B6** and **magnesium**.

LOW IN
CALORIES

LOW IN SATURATED
FAT

HIGH IN
SELENIUM

-63

CEDAR-PLANKED WILD SALMON WITH GINGER

- 1 lb. wild salmon
- 1 T extra virgin olive oil
- small piece of fresh ginger
- one lime
- one cedar plank
-         sea salt and black pepper, a pinch of each

Dry salmon with a paper towel and sprinkle the fish with salt, pepper and olive oil. Finely grate the ginger using a cheese grater and spread on the fish.

Heat a grill and place a water soaked cedar plank on the grate for 2 minutes to preheat. Place the fish on the preheated plank skin side down and cook about 15 minutes or until cooked through. Remove fish from plank, sprinkle with half the juice of a lime. Serve with the other half of the lime. This recipe goes great with grilled asparagus and wild rice.

SWEET THAI SALMON

SERVES 4

- 2 salmon fillets
- 4 T Thai sweet chili dipping sauce
- 2 T soy sauce
- 1 T grated fresh ginger
- black pepper to taste
- lemon wedges for garnish

Mix dipping sauce, soy sauce, ginger, and black pepper together. Place fish in a glass dish. Pour mixture over fish and let mari- nate several minutes to an hour. Then cook on both sides under broiler until done — you'll know because the sauce will be cara- melized.

Serve on a bed of fresh greens with chow mein noodles for the perfect Asian salad. The salmon also tastes great served cold and can be made and refrigerated ahead of time for summer al fresco dining.

SALMON AND GRAVY

SERVES 4

- 1 14 oz. can salmon
- 5 T vegetable oil
- 4 T self-rising flour
- 1 1/2 c. water
- 1/2 t salt
- 1 t black pepper

Remove all bones carefully from salmon. Coat frying pan with oil. Heat on stove top over medium heat briefly. Stir flour into hot oil. Lightly brown flour over medium heat. Stir water into browned flour, salt, and pepper to make gravy. Stir salmon into gravy, cover and warm over medium heat three more minutes until hot. Add more water if too thick.

HONEY SALMON

- 4 1-in. thick fresh salmon fillets
- 2 T extra virgin olive oil
- 1/4 c. honey
- crushed red pepper, to taste
- sea salt and pepper, a pinch each

Preheat oven to 450 degrees F. Line a baking sheet with aluminum foil. Drizzle the oil on top then place the filets on the oiled sheet. Sprinkle the seasonings over the fish and top with honey. Bake uncov- ered for 15-18 minutes or until the salm- on flakes when prodded with a fork.

SIMPLE SALMON

SERVES 4

- 4 1-in. thick fresh salmon fillets
- 1 T margarine
- 1/4 c. lemon juice

Wash fillets well with lukewarm water. Drop the margarine into a frying pan on medium heat and let it melt. Then, whisk in the lemon juice. Add the fillets one at a time, cooking about five or six minutes on each side. Spoon the lemon-butter mix- ture over the fillet while cooking as needed.

Toss the fish in with some wild rice and fresh veggies to make it a meal. Use the leftover mixture to top fillets.

SALMON WITH THAI PEANUT SAUCE

SERVES 4

- 2 lbs. salmon fillet
- 4 T creamy peanut butter
- 4 T white vinegar
- 4 T soy sauce
- 3 t honey
- 2 t garlic powder
- 1/4 t ginger powder
- cayenne pepper, to taste

Stir ingredients together well, then slath- er onto salmon that's been placed in a baking dish. Bake at 350 degrees F for approximately 15-20 minutes, depending on thickness of the fish. Garnish with pars- ley.

SALMON DELISH

SERVES 4

- 4 6-oz. fillets of wild salmon
- 1/3 c. olive oil
- 1/2 t freshly minced garlic
- 1/2 t freshly grated ginger
- 1 T organic lemon pepper seasoning

Combine all ingredients except for salm- on to create a marinade. Let salmon soak in mixture for one hour.

Arrange salmon in a single layer inside a sauté pan and pour leftover marinade on top of fish. Cook at medium heat for five to seven minutes. Turn salmon, cover pan, and turn off the burner. Let fish set for 10 minutes.

Serve with lightly sautéed asparagus and roasted rosemary cubed new potatoes.

CURRY SALMON RICE

SERVES 4-5

- 2 c. canned salmon, drained and flaked
- 1 1/2 c. rice
- 1/2 c. frozen peas, thawed
- 1/2 c. broccoli florets
- 2 T olive oil
- 2 eggs, beaten
- 2 T curry powder
- 2 T soy sauce

Rinse rice well and low boil until tender; drain any remaining water. Heat half the oil in a wok and stir fry the rice, sprinkling with curry. Add the peas, broccoli, salmon and soy sauce, and keep stir-frying for 30 seconds or until aromatic. Heat the re- maining oil in a small non-stick pan, and quickly scramble the eggs until almost set. Add the eggs to the stir fry, blending them through the mixture with a fork to break them up. Serve immediately.

SANGRIA SALMON WITH SALSA

- 4 1-in. thick salmon fillets
- sangria
- 3 medium-sized green bell peppers
- 1/2 medium-sized red onion
- 4 oz. jalapeños
- 3 large tomatoes
- lime juice

Place salmon on center of aluminum foil and bring up the sides to make a bowl around the salmon. Pour a small amount of sangria over the salmon. Chop all veg- etables and place in a bowl. Drizzle salsa with lime juice. Spoon a generous amount of salsa over the salmon. Close the foil. Place in oven at 350 degrees F for 15-20 minutes, or until fish is flaky.

KULEBIAK:
Polish Salmon Turnover

> **Note:** The Welsh have their pasties, the Italians their calzones and His- panics have empanadas. The Poles call their version of pocket meals kulebiak, while Russians call them kulebyaka.
>
> The pastry can be yeast dough, filo or puff pastry and the fillings are limited only by your imagination. Here, salmon, eggs, and rice make an elegant pescatarian meal. Add a salad or green vegetable and you've got a gourmet offering even the kids will eat! If you really want to get fancy, serve with a bechamel or white sauce.

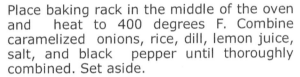

- 4 3-4-oz. skinless salmon fillets
- 1/4 c. caramelized onion
- 1 c. cooked brown rice
- 1 T chopped fresh dill
- 1 T lemon juice
- 1/4 t salt
- 1/8 t black pepper
- 1 8-oz. sheet puff pastry
- salt and black pepper, to taste
- 3 large hard-boiled eggs, chopped
- 1 beaten large egg for sealing and glazing

Place baking rack in the middle of the oven and heat to 400 degrees F. Combine caramelized onions, rice, dill, lemon juice, salt, and black pepper until thoroughly combined. Set aside.

On a parchment-paper-lined baking sheet, roll out puff pastry to a 12-in. square. Spread re- served rice mixture on half of the pastry, leav- ing a 1-in. margin around the edges.

Lay salmon fillets on top of rice. Season to taste with salt and pepper. Scatter eggs on top of salmon.

Brush pastry edges with beaten egg and flip top half of pastry over filling. Press edges together, sealing well, and crimp as for a pie.

Brush entire surface with beaten egg. Create a decorative criss-cross design, if desired, by running the back of a knife in parallel diagonal lines through the glaze. Be careful not to pierce the pastry. Using a skewer, make four tiny vent holes to allow steam to escape.

Bake 40 minutes, loosely covering top with foil after 30 minutes to prevent overbrowning. Al- low to cool before cutting into slices.

TILAPIA

Tilapia is quickly becoming one of the most popular types of seafood in the nation. This fish makes for a superlative source of phosphorus, niacin, selenium, vitamin B12, and potassium. Its natu- rally mild flavor and ability to absorb flavors while cooking make it an

ideal type of fish to serve children and picky eaters.

MILD FLAVOR

HIGH IN POTASSIUM

HIGH IN PROTEIN

SWEET AND SOUR TILAPIA

- 2 6-8-oz. tilapia fillets
- 1 T olive oil
- 1/2 medium-sized onion, chopped
- 1 small tomato, diced
- 1 T red wine vinegar
- 2 T raisins
- 1 t brown sugar
- 1 T parsley, chopped
- 2 T pine nuts, toasted
- 1/2 t salt
- black pepper, to taste

Preheat oven to 425 degrees F. Heat the olive oil in a skillet over medium heat.
Add the onion and sauté until translucent. Add the tomato, sprinkle with 1/4 t salt, and sauté three more minutes. Add vinegar, raisins, brown sugar, and anoth- er 1/4 t salt. Sauté three more minutes.

Place tilapia fillets in a roasting pan just large enough to hold them. Season with salt and pepper. Next, pour the sauce over them and bake for 20 minutes.

Sprinkle with parsley and pine nuts be- fore serving.

BLACK BEAN SALSA-TOPPED TILAPIA

- 4 6-oz. tilapia fillets
- 2 T olive oil
- 1/2 15-oz. can black beans
- 1/2 10-oz. can diced tomatoes, with Italian seasoning
- 1/2 c. fresh corn
- 2 medium-sized scallions, chopped
- salt and black pepper, to taste
- blackening season, to taste

Sauté each fillet on either side in an oil- coated pan, salting and peppering to taste. In a bowl, combine the beans, to- matoes, scallions and spices.

Serve fish on a bed of fresh spinach with a generous scoop of salsa.

LEMONY TILAPIA

- 4 6-oz. tilapia fillets
- 4 T butter, melted
- 4 T lemon juice
- 1 c. dry, seasoned stuffing
- salt and pepper, to taste

Preheat oven to 400 degrees F. Toss stuff- ing mix with the melted butter and set aside.

Wash and completely dry the tilapia fil- lets. Place tilapia on a buttered, oven- proof platter. Sprinkle fish with lemon juice, salt and peper. Cover the filets with the buttered bread crumbs.

Bake until the fish flakes easily with a fork, about 15-20 minutes.

BAKED TILAPIA WITH DILL SAUCE

SERVES 4

- 4 4-oz. tilapia fillets
- 1 T lemon pepper
- 1 T garlic powder
- 1 T onion powder
- 1 T Cajun seasoning
- 1 lemon, thinly sliced
- 1/4 c. mayonnaise
- 1/2 c. sour cream
- 1 t fresh lemon juice
- 2 T fresh dill, chopped
- salt, to taste

Preheat the oven to 350 degrees F. Season the tilapia fillets with dry mixture (lemon pepper, garlic powder, onion powder, Ca- jun seasoning, salt) on both sides. Ar- range the seasoned fillets in a single layer in the greased baking dish. Place a layer of lemon slices over the fish fillets. Bake uncovered for about 15 to 20 minutes or until fish flakes easily with a fork.

While the fish is baking, mix together the mayonnaise, sour cream, lemon juice and dill in a small bowl.

LIME BUTTER TILAPIA

- 4 1/2 lb. tilapia fillets
- 3/4 t kosher salt, divided
- 1/2 t pepper, divided
- 5 T unsalted butter, divided
- 1 T lime zest
- 1 T lime juice
- 1 shallot, chopped finely

Preheat large sauté pan on medium-high two or three minutes. Season both sides of fish with 1/2 t of the salt and 1/4 t of the pepper. Place 1 T of the butter into pan to coat it. Add fish and cook on me- dium heat three minutes on each side or until flesh is opaque and separates easily with a fork. Cook time may vary depend- ing on the thickness of the fish.

Meanwhile, cut remaining butter into small pieces and place in small bowl to soften. Add lime zest and shallots. Drizzle lime juice over fish then remove it from the pan. Stir remaining salt and pepper into softened butter mixture until well blended. Heat butter mixture in the pan to soften shallots and then spoon over fish.

SPICY TILAPIA WITH PEPPERS

SERVES 4

- 4 8-oz. tilapia fillets
- 2 medium-sized green peppers, diced
- 2 medium-sized red peppers, diced
- 1 medium-sized sweet onion, diced
- 4 T olive oil
- Creole seasoning, to taste
- 2 c. cooked rice, white or brown

Sprinkle fillets with Creole seasoning and set aside. In medium skillet, sauté veg- etables in 2 T olive oil until partially done but still crisp. Remove from pan and add another 2 T olive oil. Add fish and sauté until done, when fish is white and flakes with a fork, about eight minutes on each side. Serve at once with vegetables topped over fish and rice on the side.

BREADED TILAPIA

- 4 4-oz. tilapia fillets
- 1/2 c. panko bread crumbs
- olive oil spray
- Old Bay seasoning, to taste

Preheat oven between 375 degrees F. Coat non-stick baking tray with olive oil spray. Spray each fillet with olive oil to coat each piece. Season each fillet with your seasoning choice. Coat with bread crumbs. Place fillets on baking tray and cook 10 minutes on each side.

BAJA TILAPIA TACOS

- 1 lb. tilapia
- 1 packet taco seasoning mix
- 1 c. shredded red cabbage
- 8 soft taco-sized whole wheat tortillas
- 1 c. shredded Mexican blend cheese
- 1 c. fresh salsa
- 1/2 c. reduced-fat sour cream
- 1 T extra virgin olive oil
- fresh cilantro, chopped, to taste

Heat olive oil in a medium skillet over me- dium heat. Add fish and cook until opaque and flakey. Add in 3/4 of taco seasoning mix and water as instructions indicate on seasoning packet. Reduce heat to medium-low.

Meanwhile, mix remaining 1/4 of the sea- soning mix and sour cream together and set aside. Wrap tortillas in damp paper towels and microwave for one minute to warm. Spread one T seasoned sour cream and 1/8 cup of salsa in warm tortilla. Place 1/8 cup of the tilapia in tortilla, top with 1 oz. of cheese and 1/8 cup of cabbage, and a sprinkling of cilantro.

GARLICKY CURRY TILAPIA

SERVES 4

- 4 6-oz. tilapia fillets
- 1/4 t salt
- 1/2 t black pepper
- 1/2 t garlic salt
- 1/2 T garlic cloves, minced
- 1 T curry powder
- 1 T garlic powder
- 1 T onion powder
- 2 T olive oil
- 4 T salted butter

In a large bowl, mix together all the sea- sonings, 1 T olive oil, and butter until it becomes a paste. Then cover each fill- let with mixture. Set aside any leftover mixture and let marinated fish sit in the fridge for about 15-20 minutes.

Preheat oven to 350 degrees F. Once chilled, place marinated fish into a cast- iron skillet and put the remaining mix- ture on top of the tilapia. Cook fish for 15 minutes or until fish is flaky.

VEGGIE-TOPPED TILAPIA

SERVES 4

- 4 5-oz. tilapia fillets
- 1/3 c. white wine
- 1/2 t seafood seasoning
- 1 medium-sized onion, finely chopped
- 1 medium-sized green pepper, finely-chopped
- 1 small tomato, chopped
- 3 T fresh lemon juice
- 1 t olive oil
- 1/4 t garlic powder
- 1/4 c. shredded parmesan cheese

Place filets in a 13-in. x 9-in. baking dish coated with cooking spray. Drizzle with wine; sprinkle with seafood seasoning.

Combine the onion, green pepper, to- mato, lemon juice, oil and garlic; spoon over fillets. Cover and bake at 425 de- grees F for 15 minutes. Uncover; sprin- kle with Parmesan cheese.

Bake five to 10 minutes longer or un- til vegetables are tender and fish flakes easily with a fork.

SHRIMP

Although "shrimp" has become a synonym for "small," these crea-
tures are nothing short of high nutritional value. Eating steamed shrimp in high quantities can actually raise levels of the "good cholesterol," HDL. Shrimp are a mineral-rich shellfish, supplying
plenty of iron, zinc, and copper. They are also low in total
and saturated fat and calories.

HIGH IN ZINC

HIGH IN IRON

HAS "GOOD CHOLESTROL"

SHRIMP GAZPACHO

- 6 giant shrimp ice cold, cooked and peeled
- 6 oz. low-sodium V-8 juice
- 1 t hot sauce of your choice (optional)
- 1 t Worcestershire sauce
- 1 t chive, finely chopped

Mix all ingredients except the shrimp in a small bowl. Place the shrimp in a gob- let and pour the mixture over the shrimp.   Chill for about an hour and enjoy.

SHRIMP LINGUINE ALFREDO

SERVES 4

- 40 small shrimp (fresh or frozen)
- 1 16-oz. package of linguine pasta, cooked al dente
- 1/4 c. butter, melted
- 4 T diced onion
- 4 t minced garlic
- 1 c. half and half
- 2 t ground black pepper
- 6 T grated parmesan cheese
- 4 sprigs of parsley
- 4 slices lemon (for garnish)

While pasta is cooking, melt butter in a large saucepan. Sauté onion and gar- lic over medium heat until tender. Add shrimp and sauté over medium to high heat for one minute, stirring constantly.   Stir in half and half. Cook while stirring   constantly until sauce thickens. Place pas- ta in serving dish and cover with shrimp   and sauce. Sprinkle with black pepper and parmesan cheese. Garnish with parsley and lemon slices.

SHRIMP 'N SCALLOPS PASTA

SERVES 4

- 1 lb. shrimp, uncooked
- 1 lb. scallops
- 1/2 medium-sized green pepper, diced
- 1 T garlic , chopped
- 2 T olive oil
- 4 c. cooked pasta
- salt and pepper, to taste

Bring the olive oil to medium heat in a   skillet. Sauté the garlic and green pepper   for about five minutes. Add the scallops   and shrimp and cook an additional seven minutes, covered.

Stir the skillet mixture into the cooked pasta and place a couple scoops in a serving dish.

SAVORY SHRIMP AND GROUPER

SERVES 2

- 4 to 5 large shrimp
- 1 1-in. thick grouper filet
- 2 halved cherry tomatoes
- 2 T onions, diced
- 2 T salted butter

Arrange the shrimp on top of the grou- per filets and wrap it all up in a tin foil with the rest of the ingredients, making a loose tent. Place it on the grill and let it steam. Let it cook for about 10 minutes. You'll know it's done when the shrimp turn pink.

COD

Cod, like tilapia, is mild in flavor — tasting less "fishy" than many types of seafood. Its high levels of protein are easily absorbed in the human body. Cod's large amounts of vitamin B12 and vitamin B6 help keep homocysteine levels low, thus reducing risk for heart attack and stroke. In addition, eating cod can have anti-inflammatory effects within human skin — sometimes able to even protect against sunburn.

ANTI-INFLAMMATORY EFFECTS

HIGH IN VITAMIN B12

CAN HELP PREVENT STROKE

COLEMAN'S COD SANDWICH

- 2 lbs. cod
- 1/2 c. flour
- 1/2 c. fine cracker meal
- 16 slices of white bread
- 1 egg
- 3 c. milk
- 3/4 c. salt
- 2 1/2 T black pepper
- canola oil (for frying)

Combine the salt and black pepper in a small bowl and set aside. This is the dry seasoning mix. Whisk 1/4 c. seasoning mix you just made into the egg and milk in another bowl.

Cut the fish filets into 4-oz. portions, about 1/2-in. thick. Flour both sides of the fish fillets and dip them into the egg wash. Then dredge them in the cracker meal. Cook the filets in a small deep fryer or fry- ing pan at 350 degrees F for five minutes or until golden brown. Place each cooked filet between two slices of bread.

BAKED COD

SERVES 4

- 4 4-oz. codfish fillets
- 1/3 c. olive oil
- 2 T garlic powder
- 1 medium-sized white onion, diced
- salt and pepper, to taste

Arrange the fillets in a baking pan lined with aluminum foil. Drizzle olive oil over the fish and dust with garlic powder, salt, and pepper. Sprinkle onions on top, too. Bake covered at 375 degrees F for a total of 15 minutes.

COD FILLETS WITH RED PEPPER SAUCE

SERVES 4

- 4 4-oz. codfish fillets
- 1/2 t dried dill
- 1/2 t Dash seasoning
- 1/4 t salt
- 2 T olive oil
- 1 lime, cut into wedges
- 2 medium-sized red bell peppers, chopped
- 1/2 c. green onion, chopped
- 1 clove garlic, minced
- 1 t coriander
- 1/4 t crushed red pepper flakes

In a large skillet, sauté the onion and gar- lic in oil on medium heat about five min- utes or until tender. Add the red peppers, coriander and red pepper flakes. Sauté for one minute. Cook covered over low heat for seven to nine minutes until the peppers are soften. Add the salt to the mixture. Sprinkle the fish with the Dash seasoning and dill.

Cook the fish in the oven on 400 degrees F until opaque. This should take from eight to 10 minutes.

Serve the fish topped with the pepper sauce and lime wedges.

COD FRITTERS

- 1/2 lb. salted cod
- 1 c. flour
- 1 medium-sizedtomato chopped
- 1/2 t garlic clove, minced
- 2 scallion stalks, chopped
- 1 t baking powder
- 1/2 t adobo seasoning
- 1 c. water
- canola oil (for frying)
- hot sauce, to taste

Soak salted cod in cold water in the refridgerator for at least five hours, changing water several times prior to cooking.

Remove skin and bones from the cod. Shred it and set aside.

In a bowl, make a batter by whisking together the flour, baking powder, adobo, and water. When smooth, mix in garlic, chopped scallions, chopped tomato, and shredded fish.

In a skillet, heat 1/4-in. of oil on medium heat. Drop the batter by spoon- fuls into hot oil and cook until golden brown.

Drain fritters on paper towel, cool, and serve.

TUNA

Even two servings of tuna a week can help prevent a lot of undesirable health outcomes like low density cholesterol, stroke, obesity, type II diabetes, and several types of cancer includ- ing oral, gastric, and colon cancers. Tuna's rich concentration of folic acid and vitamin B6 can reduce homocysteine — which means less chance of atheroscleorosis, the hardening of arteries. It's also high in omega-3 and low in both carbohydrates and fat.

HIGH IN FOLIC ACID

LOW IN CARBOHYDRATES

HIGH IN VITAMIN B6

TUNA NOODLE CASSEROLE

SERVES 6

- 2 5-oz. cans of light tuna, drained
- 1 16-oz. box of macaroni shells
- 1 15-oz. can English peas, drained
- 1 10-oz. can cream of mushroom soup
- 1 1/2 c. mayonnaise
- 1 5-oz. can water chestnuts
- 1 64-oz. can sliced mushrooms
- salt and pepper, to taste

Prepare shells as box instructs. Drain the pasta once cooked, add remaining ingre- dients and stirred. Add more mayonnaise for a creamier texture. Serve either hot or cold.

TUNA SPREAD

SERVES 6

- 2 12-oz. cans of light tuna, drained
- 1 medium-sized tomato, diced
- cilantro, diced, to taste
- 1/4 red onion, diced
- 1/2 large apple, diced
- 1 small lime
- 1/4 c. sour cream
- 2 T mayonnaise
- 2 T olive oil
- salt, to taste

Use a large bowl to mix tuna with onion, tomato, cilantro, and apple. Squeeze entire lime over ingredients in the bowl. Pour olive oil over tuna mixture and salt. Finalize tuna spread by adding mayon- naise and sour cream. Mix all ingredients with a spoon and serve.

MARY HARTMAN TUNA LOAF

- 2 5-oz. cans light tuna packed, drained
- 1 1/2 c. milk
- 3/4 c. cracker crumbs (20-30 Saltine crackers, crushed)
- 4 T butter or margarine
- 2 eggs
- 1/2 t salt (optional)

Heat milk and butter in saucepan until butter melts. Add cracker crumbs.

Beat eggs and mix with tuna and salt. Add milk mixture and mix well.

Bake uncovered in a greased loaf pan at 350 degrees for one hour.

Recipe is easily doubled to bake in a 9-in. X 13-in. pan for one hour. Allow to sit for 10 minutes after removing from oven.

TUNA SALAD

- 3 5-oz. cans of low fat tuna, drained
- 1 16-oz. box of elbow noodles, cooked
- 1 medium-sized tomato, diced
- 1 medium-sized onion, diced
- 2 c. mayo
- salt and pepper, to taste

Combine all ingredients in a bowl and stir. Place in refrigerator for approximately one hour and serve.

CATFISH

Catfish is an excellent source for selenium and vitamin B12. It's also a good source for potassium and niacin. Just a 15.6 g serving of catfish provides you with the daily requirement of amino acids your body requires — this helps provide energy, build lean muscle mass, and improve immunity functions.

DAILY REQUIREMENT OF AMINO ACIDS

IMPROVES IMMUNITY FUNCTIONS

HIGH IN POTASSIUM

GRILLED CREOLE CATFISH SALAD

SERVES 2

- 2-3 medium-sized catfish fillets, cleaned and rinsed
- Creole seasoning (I use Tony Chachere's Creole Seasoning), to taste
- non-stick spray
- 2 c. romaine lettuce, chopped
- 1-2 cucumbers, sliced
- 1-2 medium-sized tomatoes, diced
- 2 hard-boiled eggs, chopped
- Italian salad dressing, to taste

Spray indoor electric grill with non-stick spray. Warm grill and place fillets on on it. Shake a generous portion of seasoning on the fish.

Cook until done — exact time depends upon the thickness of your filets. When meat becomes white and flaky, you know it's finished.

While cooking, prepare salad in individu- al bowls or plates using your favorite salad items.

When fish is done, cut into cubes and place on top of individual salads.

CHEESY SEAFOOD SPAGHETTI

SERVES 5 or 6

- 1 lb. catfish
- 1 lb. shrimp
- 1 lb. scallops
- 1/2 lb. clam (breathed overnight)
- 1 16-oz. box spaghetti, cooked
- 1 c. cheddar and mozzarella cheese, grated
- 1 medium-sized red onion, minced
- 1 clove garlic, minced
- 4 green onion stalks (for garnish)
- 1 10-oz. can cream of mushroom soup
- 2 c. 2 percent milk
- canola oil (for frying the catfish)

Wash all the seafood.

Fry the catfish golden brown in a semi-deep pan with the canola oil on medium heat.

Sauté garlic, onion, shrimp, scallop and clams (until clams are open) in olive oil in a skillet on medium heat.

Mix milk , cream of mushroom soup, and cheese. Pour the mixture over sautéed ingredients to create a sauce.

Pour the sauce over spaghetti noodles and gar- nish with minced green onion stalks be- fore serving.

OTHER FISH

LINGUINE WITH WHITE CLAM SAUCE

SERVES 4

- 1 2-oz. tin flat filet anchovies
- 2 6-oz. cans clams, minced
- 1 t dried thyme
- 1/2 t dried basil
- 1/2 t dried oregano
- 1 c. white wine
- 2 T extra virgin olive oil
- 1 T butter
- 1/2 t red pepper flakes
- 4-6 cloves garlic, minced
- 1 lemon, zested
- 1 lb. linguini, cooked al dente
- 1/4 c. chopped parsley leaves
- black pepper, to taste
- coarse salt, to taste

Heat a large non-stick skillet over medi- um heat. Add olive oil, butter, red pepper flakes, garlic, and anchovies and cook un- til anchovies melt into the oil. Add thyme, basil, oregano, wine, and clam juice. Stir in clams and lemon zest.

Add pasta to skillet and toss with sauce two to three minutes, until pasta has ab- sorbed some of the sauce and flavor. Add parsley, pepper and salt and serve.

Try with shredded or grated parmesan cheese sprinkled on top.

SARDINE SANDWICH

SERVES 1

- 1 4-oz. case sardines
- 2 slices bread, white or wheat
- hot sauce, to taste (optional)

Open the tin of sardines and arrange on one slice of bread. Douse in hot sauce, if desired. Top open-face sandwich with the other slice. Serve.

WHITEFISH WITH SAUTÉED VEGETABLES

SERVES 4

- 4 4-oz. whitefish filets
- 2 T extra virgin olive oil
- 1 red bell pepper, sliced
- 1 yellow or orange bell pepper, sliced
- 1 small white onion, diced
- 2-3 cloves garlic, minced
- 1 c. brown rice

Preheat oven to 350 degrees. Prepare cookie sheet by lining it with enough tin foil to form a 'boat' for the fish and veggies.

Heat olive oil and peppers in a large sauté pan on medium for five minutes. Add the on- ion and garlic and sauté for three more min- utes. Then cook the filets only long enough to sear both sides.

Place fish and veggies onto tin foil and fold long sides up to meet, then fold down to- gether leaving a few inches of space over the fish. Cup the edges to prevent spillage but leave some space open to allow steam to escape. Bake for 15 minutes or until fish flakes.

Prepare rice while fish is baking and serve with fish. If desired, add a splash of lemon or lime to the fish.

-83

Fish Consumption Recommendations
low   moderate   high

Women can eat up to 12 ounces per week.	Women can eat up to 4 ounces per week.	Do not eat these fish.
• catfish (farm-raised)^ • clam • cod • crab • flatfish (flounder, plaice, sole) • haddock • herring^ • mackerel (Atlantic, jack, chub)^ • mullet • oyster (cooked) • pollock • rainbow trout • salmon (wild, farm-raised)^ • sardines^ • scallops • shad^ • shrimp • squid • tilapia • tuna (canned Skipjack, light) • whitefish^ • whiting ^ high in healthy omega-3 fatty acids	• bass (saltwater, black) • buffalo fish • carp • grouper • halibut • lobster (northern, Maine, Atlantic) • mahi mahi (dolphin-fish) • perch (freshwater) • pompano • sablefish • sea trout (weakfish) • Spanish mackerel (S. At- lantic) • tilefish (Atlantic) • tuna (canned albacore, yellowfin, or white) • white croaker (Pacific)	• bass (striped)* • bluefish * • Chilean sea bass • golden snapper • jack (Amberjack, Crevalle) • king mackerel • marlin • orange roughy • sea lamprey • shark • Spanish mackerel (Gulf of Mexico) • swordfish • tilefish (Gulf of Mexico) • tuna (all fresh or frozen) • walleye (Great Lakes) * PCB (polychlo-rinated biphenyls) are higher in these species
LOW IN MERCURY	**MODERATE IN MERCURY**	**HIGH IN MERCURY**

HOW MUCH FISH TO EAT?

Health experts recommend that women eat 8-12 oz. per week and children (ages 2-6) eat 2 oz. of fish low in mercury per week. As a good rule of thumb, keep in mind that three ounces of fish is about the size of a deck of cards.

FILL IN THE <u>BLANK</u>

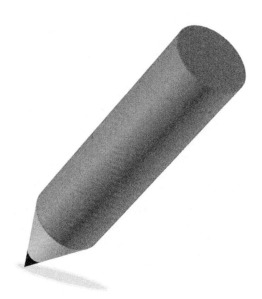

Fishing can be_____!

Fishing if fun for me and my _____.

Fishing can be _____ sometimes.

Fishing with a _____is fun.

Fishing at night is _____.

My family likes to fish every_____.

I love to catch _____fish.

I never leave_____ on my fish.

My dad looks cool when he is _____.

I always catch _____fish all the time.

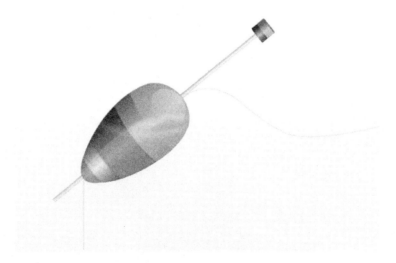

My father can catch fish very _____.

My brother likes to fish _____.

I like to watch big _____.

This fish just had a birthday _____.

Complete the dot to dot drawing

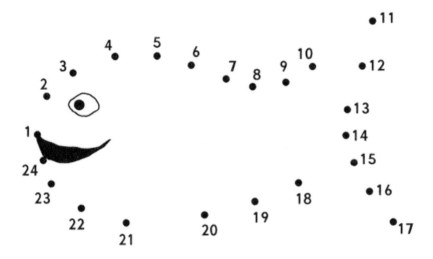

Disclaimer Statement